# MORE THAN
## *She's*
# EVER KNOWN

An ailing senior and her journey
to comfort and peace

A daughter assisting her mother to
Salvation for her final days

BY

STEPHANIE CLARKE PELTON

**PRESS**

*I* always knew she loved me. For well over 50 years now, I never doubted any day of my life that she was driven to be the best Mom. Her best was all she had known. From a complacent upbringing, with a beautiful roof over her head and her parents' love, her circumstances led to defining moments. In the end, she gave all three of her children unconditional love, which was all she ever knew.

Mom was a submissive wife; I recall this growing up. She was certainly the most beautiful. Her hair flowing and makeup always perfect, she had an extravagant closet full of the best clothing. Her casual attire was sleek; her formal wear was captivating. She was always on call for beauty, as she remained proud of being on a professional athlete's arm.

The years progressed; during my development into a woman, mom and I remained the best together, especially through the difficult times. We endured what we felt were compiled tragedies, depression, loneliness and fear together. We always had the most profound love and support for one another. This was good and truly needed, because we had no idea what was yet to come. We were about to experience the most frightening, yet meaningful times in our lives.

### The Aging Parent

$\mathcal{T}$ime brought chronic conditions, severe illnesses and disabilities leading to confinement. Our family was forced to utilize a nursing facility for mom's care. This time of crisis was devastating: accepting my loved one, my parent my Mother, my morning glory had to be succumbed to the care of strangers. This moment was profoundly humbling.

*I*t was difficult accepting our loved ones as literally helpless in the care of others who were merely doing a job where money is no reward. These caregivers can appear without compassion, stone-faced and heartless, yet there are blessings in these facilities. They contain competencies we as family just cannot provide daily, but also the guilt a family member feels leaving them alone each day. The guilt I struggled with was ruthless; extremely painful. I stayed on the edge, worried and torn. I wanted Mom with me, but realistically I knew she was very sick and this was no longer possible.

om's voice was always heard, always strong. Her mindset was amazing; she always knew the meds and dosage that were prescribed, she knew what time her body needed some type of relief. She remained in such pain; she stayed so alert that she challenged the staff often, especially in areas she found them to be mindless. I stayed in support of her always and met with Directors often.

*P*lease make sure you establish respect with your loved one's facility. Mom wanted these words expressed; she wanted proper care for our ailing seniors. I soon realized mom was on her own mission.

She was born 73 years ago in a very small city in Illinois. She had a beautiful mixed heritage. She remained vibrate, inquisitive, very smart, a bit of a loner, always loving the elders. She married the man of her dreams, her prince charming: breathtakingly handsome and a professional in many ways. He became father to her three children. Beautiful family; happy life. Mom played the role of wife, the homemaker supporting her family in these roles in the most beautiful environments. Luxury was always vital and love unconditional.

One of mom's biggest tests was becoming her own head of household after divorce. She had to work and maintain her family. During this time she went to school studied to receive her GED; we actually graduated from high school during the same year. I don't think I ever told her how proud I was of her. How could I at 18 years of age? I had no idea; I was too self-centered then. My next book...

Mom remained single through the years, in constant communication with her children. She was blessed with beautiful grandchildren and great grandchildren, as well as a former husband loving her from afar.

## *Then My Hardship Began*

On January 16, 2010 Mom passed over to The Kingdom of Heaven. I said goodbye to by far the most amazing woman in my life. The last years spent with her were extraordinary; these writings are dedicated to Mom as her memory lives within me. They are shared so you can experience the beautiful journey that manifested in her to reach Salvation. This gave Mom the most amazing peace during the final days of her earthly existence.

*M*om wanted all beautiful seniors suffering physically and mentally, worn out living in nursing facilities, to find peace and place all their thoughts, dreams and desires on the beauty and glory of God in all that cannot be seen.

*S*he gave me way too much credit as He lived through me for her. I taught Mom not to lose hope as her physical body was becoming older and weaker. Our spirits inside us are renewed every day. Mom knew we have small troubles for now, but they are helping us gain eternal glory that is much greater than our troubles. We learn to set our eyes not on what we see, but on what we cannot see – what is seen is only for a while, but what is unseen will last forever!

*My Journey, My Personal Storm*

The path of witnessing my beautiful mother getting older in a nursing home – so frail, changing, deteriorating right before me – pained me beyond words. The wonderment in her touch, yet with hands always so cold now, the loving embrace from her wheelchair... there is nothing like a mother's arms around you. How much she loved me, how much she stayed mesmerized by my Alex. Her grandson's prayers brought her so much comfort as he always prayed over her before we left the facility; her love for him was so massive, so deep.

### Mom's Diagnosis

*I* recall meeting with home health care consultants 10 years before mom became so ailed; their words were as accurate as her condition and its demise. Lupus, Chronic Obstructive Pulmonary Disease (COPD), Osteoporosis and heart disease took Mom's life at only 73 years of age though women in this generation live so much longer. My mother's mother lived well into her 90s, along with a sister who was well in her 80s before death. The last survivor is my aunt in Illinois. She is such a stronghold for us all; I thank God that she remains the beautiful voice in our family and sustains unconditional love for us all.

Mom's reward was Heaven's gain; the Lord God put her earthly existence, her pain and suffering to an end. My only satisfaction is knowing she hurts no more. Not having the daily interaction is still quite difficult, but Mom is gone. Heaven is now her home...

When the time comes for you to make decisions for an ailing parent, consider caregivers or turn to a nursing home, only then will you realize the hardships this role will encompass. One of the most difficult realizations was that I could not rescue her. I knew each and every day Mom had to adjust to her own environment. I had to accept her body was changing for the worse; physicians confirmed she would not get better.

*H*ow do you comfort yourself along with your dying loved one? You insist on prayer, leading them to God the Father, ensuring there is peace and comfort allowing them to handle another day and the next day all over again. Seniors thrive off of routine; Mom had hers; yours will have theirs. In the interim, make sure you love them unconditionally.

*Mom's Favorite Prayer*

The Prayer of Jabez: "Oh that you would Bless me indeed and enlarge my territory; that your hand would be with me and that you would keep me from evil and that I may not cause pain." This prayer brought so much hope for her during the difficult times of confinement in the nursing facility. It is by far one of the most depressing places to witness, the most lonely environment family members observe. On occasion I would think loved ones are much better off when they are not of sound mind and body so they don't endure what could actually happen that is so treacherous.

*I* would receive phone calls from Mom, in tears and unable to cope with the insensitivity of onsite med aids or staff. Unfortunately, the burdens or personal circumstances that the facility staff was carrying festered over to our loved ones on occasion. Listen, be the support factor for your parent. Try not to make judgments on the circumstances and just wait for the storm to pass, making sure there is no physical harm.

Our seniors ailed – afraid, angry, depressed and in enormous pain – subjected to all sorts of behavior. It is that you stay close to your confined parent and establish relationships with the nurses and med staff on your loved one's team. You will gain much respect if you stay active with visits.

Our strength stayed in the Lord. Tears held high, we knew all we had was prayer and Mom became quite an amazing grace! These last writings were prayers and scriptures from my beautiful Mother, Sandy. In prayer we said, "Lord the one you love is sick; the one you love is tired, sad, lonely, fearful, depressed."

The Savior hears the prayer; He silences Heaven so He won't miss a word and He hears the Prayer. "When you're in trouble, remember I'm present to help. Give Me your burdens and I will sustain you. When you are stressed out and worn down by the pressures of life, lean on Me. I will be your rock, your fortress, your deliverer and your strength. Even though you may fail from time to time, you won't be discarded because I am upholding you. However, a word of caution: take no advice from those who are spiritually blind. Delight yourself in My word." We have known and believed the love that God has for us. God is love and he who abides in love abides in God and God in him.

*God Shall Send Forth His Mercy and Truth*

# *Psalm 57:1*

"Be merciful unto me O God; be merciful unto me for my soul trusteth in thee. Yea, in the shadows of thy wings will I make my refuge until these calamities be overpassed."

"Ask," promised Jesus, "and it will be given to you." Live in God's word; keep speaking it over your situation and it will work. "In everything give thanks for this is the will of God." Complaining robs me of God's blessings. Pray bold prayers (Psalm 28)! Pray about your deepest hopes, greatest dreams and desires.

*Anxious About Your Health?*

## Read these scriptures.

1) "Worship the Lord your God and His blessing will be on your food and water. I will take away sickness from among you, I will give you a full life span."

2) "'I will restore you to health and heal your wounds,' declares the Lord."

3) "Listen closely to my words; do not let them out of your sight, keep them within your heart for they are life to those who find them and health to a man's whole body. Therefore I will tell you whatever you ask for in prayer believe that you have received it and it will be yours."

My most powerful weapon is God's Word, learn to use it, Live in God's Word, keep speaking it over my situation and it will work. Show gratitude. Set your minds on the things above. Meditate on these things, the positive things of God, what so ever are true, noble, just, pure and lovely and of good report. Engage my mind in thoughts of joy, peace, victory and abundance of blessings. Keep my mind set on the good things of God, Higher things of God.

"*The* secret things belong to the Lord our God, but those things which are revealed belong to us."

God, bless me every day and while You are at it, bless me a lot! God's nature is to bless.

*Let God's Word Settle It!*

You say, "It's impossible." God says, "With me all things are possible."
(Luke 18:27)

You say, "I'm exhausted". God says, "Wait on me, I will renew your strength."
(Isaiah 40:31)

You say, "Nobody loves me." God says, "I have loved you with an everlasting love."
(Jeremiah 31:3)

You say, "I can't go on." God says, "My grace is sufficient for you."
(2 Corinthians 12:19)

You say, "I don't know what to do." God says, "I'll direct you."
(Proverbs 3:6)

You say, "I can't do it." God says, "You can do all things through me."
(Philippians 4:13)

You say, "It's not worth it." God says, "It will be; just keep going."
(Galatians 6:9)

You say, "I can't forgive myself." God says, "You can, because I have."
(Ephesians 4:32)

You say, "I can't make ends meet." God says, "I will supply all your needs."
(Philippians 4:19)

You say, "I'm afraid." God says, "I didn't give you the spirit of fear, but of power."
(2 Timothy 1:7)

You say, "I can't handle this." God says, "Give it to me; I will carry it for you."
(Psalm 55:22)

You say, "I'm not smart enough." God says, "I'll give you wisdom."
(1 Corinthians 1:30)

You say, "I'm all alone." God says, "I will never leave you or forsake you."
(Hebrews 13:5)

*F*aith is the simplest, plainest thing in the world. It simply believes in God. When your faith feels shaky, pray: "Lord Jesus, I have placed my trust in You. Your word says I know have eternal life and it is not a matter of feeling, thinking, or wishing, it's a matter of believing and knowing I have kept your word! I choose to doubt my doubts trust in You! Amen."

*God Will Tell You What to Say*

*J*esus said: "Don't worry about how to respond of what to say, God gives the right words at the right time. For its not you who will be speaking- it will be the Spirit of your Father speaking through you" (Matthew 10:19, TLB). Stop trying to figure out in advance everything you need to say and do in every situation; you'll wear yourself out trying to prepare for every circumstance you're likely to run into.

*H*is indwelling Holy Spirit guided and protected us in each situation that arose. When we have to make hard decisions, solve complicated problems or confront difficult people, God's Spirit will decide the proper time and the best approach. He will also give us the right words to say; until then we don't need to bother ourselves with it.

*I*f we listen to what the Lord is telling us here in this passage, not only will we have more peace, but we will also enjoy more success. When we do have to speak, what comes out of our mouths will be spiritual wisdom from God and not something we have come up with out of our own carnal minds. Your responsibility is not to know the future, it's to trust in God who holds the future and be confident that you are safe in His hands.

Crown of favor on my head
I thank God His Light shines on me
Thank you that Your favor stands out all
around me
I walk in God's Favor
I declare over my life, I put faith out there
I become more favor-minded
I declare God's favor every day!

Peace to those on whom His favor rests.

Father, I thank you that I have found your favor.

Strong faith releases the greatness of God.

Extension of the Life of Jesus Christ

Exhibition of His Character

Demonstration of His power will make an impact in your life.

"That ye might walk worthy of the Lord unto all pleasing being fruitful in every good work and increasing in the knowledge of God." (Colossians 1:10)

*Increasing in the Knowledge of God*

To experience the power of God, the Holy Spirit needs do the will of God inside us all. Practice this prayer.

Transforms Life Prayer for Children

"May you be strengthened with all might according to his glorious power unto all patience and longsuffering with joyfulness."

(Colossians 1:11)

*Strong Faith is a Gift Given by God*

*B*lessed are those who have learned to walk in the light of Your presence is our source of blessings and favor.

The blessing!

Thank God for the Blessing of my life; when getting up; I walk in the fullness of God's blessing. This has given me favor in unprecedented ways.

Amen!

In Loving Memory of
Sandra Anita Blake Clarke
1936-2010

# Footnotes

**Sibling Support-**

If you have sibling support be sure and be clear on whom will be responsible for the various needs of the aging parent, if you are alone with this task best wishes it is so time consuming yet vital. In a perfect world let's ask the men to be there for Dad and woman there for Mom in personal matters but it seldom works this way. Have meetings often with siblings to discuss roles that you'll find quite necessary.

Try and keep your guilt level in tack especially if you find Nursing Home Care is best, just remember to stay visible, get to know your staff and directors caring for your parent. Make sure there is a living will and advanced directive available you are often asked if these forms are in tack.

You must handle choosing a funeral home believe me once your loved one passes over to The Kingdom all you make is one call and the provider you choose will take it from there picking up your loved ones body instantaneously then you proceed with the next steps required.

Plan your Hospice of choice, there are many variables. We found when Mom was sick at the hospital and the doctor placed her on Hospice Care, Mom did not have to leave the facility she wanted to pass over in the hospital rather than being transferred to the Nursing Home, You will have that option as well, Mom was gone less than a week later. With Hospice make sure and get clarity on when you will no longer be able to communicate with your loved one, I was not informed and was quite devastated once I realized this, and physicians can give you information on this extremely sensitive matter.

Who will oversee the parent's bills? Someone will need access to the banking account.

Caregiving like parenting will not be easy so build your foundation strong now and remember your aging parent took good care of you the best they knew how and now the role has changed so adult children be on your best behavior in Love remembering to Honor Thy Father and Thy Mother.

**Role Reversal-**

The most traumatic by far is watching a parent no longer able to take care of themselves...

Your role now as the adult child will be to oversee full time care in your home or theirs making sure your parent is fed, cleaned well, proper rest, and accompanied to doctor appointments. You may also begin to notice more frequent overnight stays at the hospital.

You as the adult child must oversee proper med care for your aging parent, if you have multiple doctors you will have multiple medications that must be over seen properly by you, I suggest compiling a binder to keep everything logged.

While they are able to communicate find out their

wishes for burial plans. The best medicine for your aging parent whether they are living with you or in a nursing facility is acceptance in this new journey for the family, pay close attention, never stop communicating. And LOVE them as your parent.

The Greatest of them all is LOVE!

CPSIA information can be obtained
at www.ICGtesting.com
Printed in the USA
LVOW12s0417300716
498235LV00001B/1/P